FOREWORD

More and more owners each year are taking advantage of the outstanding ride comfort of their Land Rovers and Range Rovers and are realising the off road potential of their vehicles.

Obviously, more stress is imposed upon a vehicle that is being driven off road, but the effect of this can be minimised by the use of correct driving techniques, which will also result in reduced driver fatigue.

This booklet is intended as a guide to the more important aspects of off road driving, but the techniques described on the following pages will, with practice, enable the Land Rover driver to extract maximum benefit from the vehicle.

It should be remembered that any vehicle is only as good as the ability of the driver, whose responsibility it is to know the vehicle and to ensure that it is properly maintained, and thus benefit from Land Rovers' many advantages.

RANGE ROVER and LAND ROVER

RECOMMENDED DRIVING PROCEDURES

The following notes are intended as a guide to Land Rover and Range Rover drivers in order that they may obtain maximum benefit from their vehicles when driving on or off road. This publication describes the basic techniques which apply to vehicles with automatic or manual transmission.

PERMANENT FOUR WHEEL DRIVE
Range Rover 5 speed
Land Rover One Ten & Ninety 5 speed

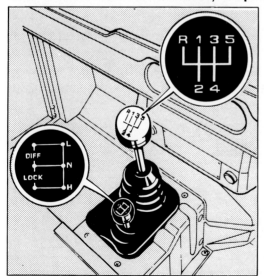

The Land Rover One Ten and Ninety feature permanent four wheel drive as standard equipment with a lockable centre differential. The differential is locked by moving the transfer lever to the left of the gate in high or low range without depressing the clutch pedal. A fascia mounted warning light indicates when the differential is locked. Low range is engaged by bringing the vehicle to a standstill and pushing the transfer lever forward through the neutral position into low range.

Re-selecting high range would normally be done with the vehicle stationary, but if it is necessary to make the change on the move, the correct procedure should be followed as detailed in the section for towing.

1

Range Rover 4 speed,
Land Rover V8 & One Ten V8 4 speed

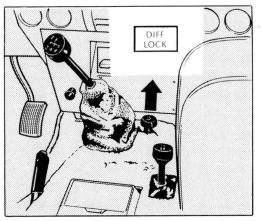

Range Rover 4 speed and all V8 Land Rovers have permanent four wheel drive transmission using lockable centre differential to prevent transmission wind up. This differential is locked by operating a tunnel mounted switch on the Range Rover and a similar switch on the V8 Land Rover which is mounted on the seat box below the centre seat position. The differential lock can be operated at any speed and it is not necessary to depress the clutch. A fascia mounted warning light indicates when the differential is locked.

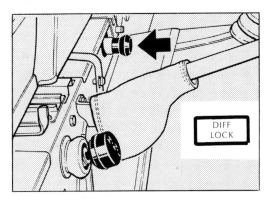

Low range is engaged by bringing the vehicle to a stop and pushing the transfer lever forward on the Range Rover, and down on the V8 Land Rover.

Range Rover Automatic — 4 speed

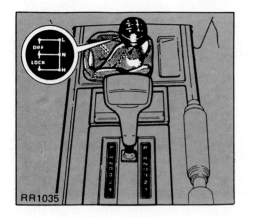

RR1035

The transfer gear lever controls the selection of the high and low gear ratios and the engagement of the differential lock.

To change ratio from high to low, or low to high, proceed as follows:

1. Reduce the vehicle speed to below 8 km/h (5 mph).
2. Move the automatic gearbox selector lever to the N neutral position.
3. Just before the vehicle comes to rest, move the transfer gear lever rapidly to the required position.

To change ratio with the vehicle stationary, simply move the automatic gearbox selector to the N (neutral) position before moving the transfer gear lever to the required position.

If the transfer gear cannot be engaged due to transmission wind-up, the following procedure should be used. Apply footbrake and handbrake, keep constant pressure on the transfer gear lever in the direction required and move the automatic gearbox selector lever rapidly from Drive, through Neutral to Reverse and back into Drive until the transfer lever is shifted. Repeat the procedure if necessary.

To change from Neutral to High or Low: Stop the vehicle and select High or Low as required. If selection proves difficult, select Park on the automatic gearbox, restart the engine, apply brakes, keep constant pressure on the transfer gear lever in the direction required and move the automatic gearbox selector rapidly between Park and Reverse until selection is made.

Range Rover Automatic — 3 speed

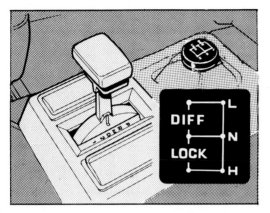

On models fitted with automatic transmission the centre differential lock control is incorporated in the transfer lever and the differential is locked by moving the transfer lever across the gate to the left. A fascia mounted warning light indicates when the centre differential is locked.

When making transfer changes between high and low ranges the following procedure is recommended:- The vehicle speed should be reduced to under 5 mph (8 kph) and the main selector lever should be moved into the neutral position. The transfer lever should be moved rapidly into the required position and then the appropriate gear should be re-engaged with the main selector lever. Alternatively, with the vehicle stationary and the brakes applied, move the main selector lever between Drive and Reverse whilst applying steady pressure to the transfer lever to engage high or low range.

SELECTABLE FOUR WHEEL DRIVE

Series III Land Rover

Selectable four wheel drive is fitted as basic equipment to Series III Land Rovers. These vehicles are driven in two wheel drive high range under normal conditions, and four wheel drive and/or low range can be engaged when the ground conditions become difficult.

4 Wheel Drive – High Range :-

Four wheel drive high range is engaged by pushing down the lever with the yellow knob and this can be done without stopping the vehicle or depressing the clutch. Two wheel drive is regained by stopping the vehicle and pulling back the lever with the red knob (transfer lever) until the lever with the yellow knob returns to the two wheel drive position, then returning the transfer lever to its original position.

4 Wheel Drive – Low Range:-

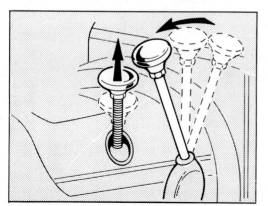

Low range is engaged by bringing the vehicle to a complete standstill and then pulling the transfer lever back through the neutral position into low range. This also engages four wheel drive. High range is regained by returning the transfer lever to the fully forward position. This change is usually carried out with the vehicle stationary although it can be made on the move and this technique is fully described in the section covering towing.

CORRECT GEAR SELECTION

Differential Lock and Four Wheel Drive

The centre differential lock on permanent four wheel drive vehicles and the four wheel drive control on all other models should be engaged whenever rough, slippery, loose or uneven terrain is encountered. Both of these controls can be operated while the vehicle is moving but not if individual wheels are already spinning due to loss of traction, and in these circumstances the vehicle should be brought to a stop. Neither four wheel drive or the centre differential lock should be engaged on hard roads except under very slippery conditions as the differential speeds of rotation of the road wheels when cornering can cause transmission damage.

If the vehicle is fitted with free-wheel front hubs, they must be locked prior to engaging four wheel drive.

Low Range

Low range should only be selected for extreme off road conditions where progress in high range could not be maintained, or in any situation where low speed manoeuvring is necessary i.e. reversing a trailer or negotiating a boulder strewn river bed. In addition, when towing a heavy load it is often easier to move off in low range and then change into high range when a reasonable road speed has been achieved. Before driving through difficult ground conditions, select low range, remembering to engage the diff lock on permanent four wheel drive vehicles, and a suitable gear; in most conditions second or third gears on vehicles fitted with manual transmission, or 'D' on vehicles fitted with automatic transmission. Only experience will tell the driver which is the correct gear for a given section of ground, but generally with manual transmission, the higher the gear, the better. Do not change gear while negotiating difficult terrain as the drag at the wheels may cause the vehicle to stop when the clutch is depressed and difficulty may be experienced in restarting.

Exercise care when using the accelerator as sudden power surges may induce wheel spin.

As the ground conditions become less difficult, high range should be reselected remembering to remain in four wheel drive or to keep the differential lock engaged where there is any risk of losing traction.

SURVEY ON FOOT BEFORE DRIVING

Before negotiating a difficult section of terrain, it is a wise precaution to carry out a preliminary survey of the ground on foot in order to minimise the risk of getting caught in a previously unnoticed hazard.

Before driving through a difficult section, select low range and a suitable gear. For most purposes second or third gears will prove practical. Only experience will tell the driver which is the correct gear for a given section but generally the higher the gear, the better.

RIDING THE CLUTCH

This will result in premature clutch wear and could result in the driver losing control of the vehicle by inadvertently depressing the clutch as the vehicle travels over a sudden bump.

BRAKING

Keep the application of the brake pedal to an absolute minimum. Braking on wet, muddy or loose surface slopes will almost certainly cause one or more wheels to lock and the resulting slide could prove dangerous.

ENGINE BRAKING

Before descending steep slopes, stop the vehicle and engage first gear low range on vehicles fitted with manual transmission or first gear hold in low range on automatic vehicles. While descending the slope it should be remembered that the engine will provide sufficient braking effort to control the speed of descent, and that the brakes should not be applied as this may cause the trailing wheels to lock on loose or slippery surfaces resulting in loss of control.

DRIVING ON SOFT GROUND

When driving through soft ground conditions, reduced tyre pressures will increase the contact area of the tyres with the ground. This will improve traction by increasing tyre flotation. It should be born in mind that reduced tyre pressures also reduce ground clearance and this could cause problems on deeply rutted tracks. The tyre pressures must be returned to normal as soon as possible. Refer to the vehicle instruction manual for advice on maximum and minimum tyre pressures.

DRIVING ON ROUGH TRACKS

Although rough tracks can be negotiated in two wheel drive, it is advisable to select four wheel drive if there is excessive suspension movement as this may induce wheel spin. On Range Rovers and Land Rovers fitted with permanent four wheel drive the centre differential should be locked.

As the track becomes rougher it may be necessary to engage low range to enable a steady low speed to be maintained without constant use of the brake and clutch pedals.

CLIMBING STEEP SLOPES

When climbing or descending slopes it is important to follow the fall line, as travelling diagonally may result in the vehicle sliding broadside down the slope. When climbing steep slopes, particularly if the surface is loose or slippery, the higher the gear used, the better, because this enables the driver to take advantage of vehicle momentum. Too much speed when climbing a hill with a bumpy surface can result in one or more wheels lifting causing the vehicle to lose traction and stop. In this case a slower approach may be more successful. Often traction can be improved by easing off the accelerator just before loss of forward motion.

1) If the vehicle fails to climb a hill but does not stall, the following procedure, which applies to vehicles fitted with automatic or manual transmission, should be adopted:–

a) Hold the vehicle on the foot brake. It will be necessary to use the handbrake only if the foot brake fails to hold due to wet brake linings.

b) Engage reverse gear low range as quickly as possible.

c) Release the brakes and clutch simultaneously.

d) Allow the vehicle to reverse down the slope using engine over run braking to control the speed of descent.

e) Do not apply the brake pedal during the descent. Even a light application may cause the front wheels to lock and this would render the steering ineffective.

2) If the engine stalls while climbing the hill, the following procedure is recommended on vehicles fitted with manual transmission.

a) Hold the vehicle on the foot brake/hand brake.

b) Engage reverse gear low range and remove feet from brake and clutch pedals.

c) Start the engine in gear and allow the vehicle to reverse down the hill using engine over run braking to check the speed. A laden vehicle on a steep hill will start without the aid of the starter motor as soon as the brakes are released, if there is sufficient traction.

When back on level ground or where traction can be regained a faster approach and the resulting extra momentum will probably enable the hill to be climbed.

d) If the engine should stall on a vehicle fitted with automatic transmission, the brakes should be applied and the engine must be restarted before reversing down the hill as there will be no braking effort from the gearbox unless the engine is running.

One Ten & Ninety

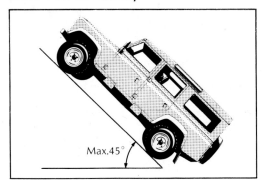

Max.45°

GROUND CLEARANCE

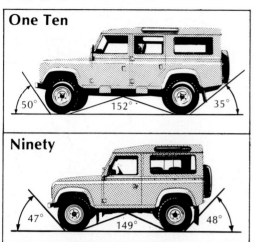

One Ten
50°   152°   35°

Ninety
47°   149°   48°

Remember the importance of maintaining ground clearance under the chassis and axle differentials and the necessity for clear approach and departure angles. Avoid deep wheel ruts, sudden changes in slope and obstacles which may foul the chassis or axles. On soft ground the axle differentials will clear their own patch in all but the most difficult conditions. However, on frozen, rocky or dry, hard ground, hard contact between the differentials and the ground will generally result in the vehicle coming to a sudden stop.

EXISTING WHEEL TRACKS

Avoid over-steering while driving along rutted tracks. This could result in the vehicle being driven on full left or right hand lock in the ruts. This must be avoided as it causes drag at the front wheels and is extremely dangerous because it can result in the vehicle suddenly veering off the track when the front wheels reach level ground or traction is found.

NEGOTIATING A
'V' SHAPED GULLY

This should be tackled with extreme caution, as steering up one or other of the gully walls could lead to the vehicle being trapped with its side against the gully wall.

CROSSING A RIDGE

Always approach a ridge at right angles so that both front wheels and then both rear wheels cross together. If approached at an angle traction can be lost completely through diagonally opposite wheels lifting off the ground.

CROSSING A DITCH

Ditches should always be crossed at an angle so that three wheels maintain contact with the ground assisting the passage of the fourth wheel through the ditch. If approached straight on, both front wheels will drop into the ditch probably with the chassis and the front bumper trapped on opposite sides of the ditch.

TRAVERSING A SLOPE

Traversing a slope should be undertaken having observed the following precautions:–

a) Check that the terrain is firm under all wheels and that the ground is not slippery.

b) Check that the downhill wheels are not likely to drop into a sudden depression in the ground as this will suddenly increase the angle of tilt.

c) For the same reason ensure that the uphill wheels do not run over rocks, tree roots, or similar obstacles.

d) Any load carried in the back of the vehicle should be evenly distributed as low as possible and made secure. A sudden shift of load while traversing a slope could cause the vehicle to overturn. Passengers in the rear should sit on the uphill side.

WADING

The maximum advisable fording depth is approximately 0.5 metres. Before negotiating a deep water crossing ensure that the clutch housing drain plug is in position, and if the water depth exceeds 0.5 metres removing the fan belt will eliminate the risk of the cooling fan spraying water over the ignition system and air cleaner. If, for various reasons, it is not possible to remove the fan belt, a sheet of plastic or other water resistant material draped in front of the radiator grille to prevent any water from passing through will reduce the risk of saturation of the ignition system.

Land Rover customers throughout the world frequently travel through water where the depth exceeds 0.5m having taken the following precautions:–

a) Generally stagnant water is more likely to be a hazard than a river or stream as flowing water tends to prevent a build up of silt. The silt in a stagnant pool can be several feet deep. Always ensure that the river or pool bed is firm enough to support the weight of the vehicle and provide traction.

b) Ensure that the engine air intake is kept clear of the water.

c) A low gear is desirable and sufficient throttle should be maintained to avoid stalling the engine if the exhaust is under water.

d) Slow steady progress should be maintained to create a bow wave.

AFTER WADING

Make sure that the brakes are dried out as soon as possible so that they are effective when needed. This can be achieved by driving for a short distance with the brakes applied.

Refit the fan belt, remove the clutch housing drain plug and any covering material from the front of the radiator grille. If the water was particularly muddy it is possible that the radiator may be blocked with mud and leaves and this should be cleared immediately to reduce the risk of overheating.

If deep water is regularly negotiated it would be wise to check all transmission oils for signs of water contamination after each trip. Emulsified oil can be easily recognised by its milky appearance.

SOFT DRY SAND

It is generally advisable when driving in soft sand to use low range as this will enable you to accelerate through suddenly worsening conditions without the risk of being unable to restart, having stopped to change from high to low range.

Remember in soft conditions that reduced tyre pressures will increase the contact area with the ground but reference should first be made to the owners manual to ascertain the correct tyre pressures for the prevailing conditions. If the tyre pressures have been reduced for soft ground conditions they must be re-inflated upon regaining firm ground.

On vehicles fitted with manual transmission, gear changing should be kept to a minimum as depressing the clutch to change gear in soft sand will cause the vehicle to stop because of the drag at the wheels.

Vehicles fitted with three speed automatic transmission are best driven in these conditions in low range with the main selector lever in the second gear hold position, as this will eliminate unnecessary automatic gear changes which would make steady progress difficult to maintain.

When stopping your vehicle in sand remember that re-starting while facing up a slope is almost impossible and you should therefore park on level ground, or with the vehicle facing down hill. In order to avoid wheel spin a standing start is best achieved using second or third gear on manual transmission vehicles, and the minimum throttle opening that is necessary to start moving.

If forward motion is lost do not try to accelerate out of trouble as this can only make things worse. Clear the sand from the tyres and ensure that the chassis and axles are not touching the sand.

If the wheels have sunk deep into the sand it will be necessary to lift the vehicle using an air bag or high lift jack and then build up the sand under the wheels so that the vehicle, when lowered, will be on level ground. If a restart is still not possible it may be necessary to place sand mats or ladders beneath the wheels.

ICE AND SNOW

Land Rovers and Range Rovers are used extensively in snow and icy conditions and the driving techniques employed are generally similar to those used for driving on mud or wet grass. Select the highest gear possible in four wheel drive and drive away using the minimum throttle opening. Avoid violent movements of the steering wheel and keep braking to a minimum. The centre differential should be locked. Do not brake hard and drive slowly.

TOWING

When preparing the vehicle and trailer the following procedure should be adhered to:–

a) Adjust vehicle tyre pressures as recommended in the owners' manual.

b) Adjust trailer tyre pressures as recommended by the trailer manufacturer.

c) Balance the trailer and the vehicle, both unladen, so that with the trailer level, the drawbar is at the same height as the hitch point on the vehicle.

On vehicles fitted with 5 speed gearboxes and manual transmission, a smooth start will be achieved when towing trailers weighing more than 2000 kg (4400 lb) by moving off in low range and then changing to high range on the move. The following procedure is recommended to avoid damage to the gearbox:–

a) Move off in first or second gear low range and increase the speed by changing through the gears to 25 - 30 km/h (15 - 20 mph).

b) Depress the clutch and move the transfer lever into neutral.

c) Remove your foot from the clutch pedal and allow the engine revs to drop to no more than 1000 rpm.

d) Depress the clutch pedal fully and immediately move the transfer lever into high range.

e) Select a gear suitable for the road speed obtained with the main gear lever.

The technique on vehicles fitted with V8 engines and 4 speed gearboxes is similar to above, the difference being that it is necessary to put the main lever into neutral before changing into high range.

On Range Rovers fitted with the automatic transmission the following procedure should be followed:–

a) Move off in low range with the main gear elector in 'D'.

b) Accelerate to approximately 8km/h (5mph) then move the main gear selector into neutral.

c) Move the transfer lever rapidly from low range into high range.

d) Re-select 'D' with the main gear selector.

It is advisable to practice the above procedures with the vehicle stationary before attempting it with the vehicle moving.

DO NOT

a) The four wheel drive and differential lock controls should be engaged before driving onto any surface where traction may be lost at one or more wheels. Do not operate either of these controls while individual wheels are spinning.

b) Do not engage low range while the vehicle is moving.

c) Do not apply the handbrake while the vehicle is moving.

d) Do not allow the engine to labour in too high a gear.

e) Do not overload the vehicle for sustained cross country work. Reduce the payload by 90kg (198lbs).

f) Do not wrap your thumbs round the steering wheel as severe steering kick back over rough ground may result in a broken thumb.

g) Do not use the clutch pedal as a foot rest. Keep the left foot well clear of the clutch pedal while the vehicle is in motion.

h) Do not rely on the handbrake to hold the vehicle if the brake linings have been subjected to immersion in mud and water.

i) Do not engage the differential lock or four wheel drive on the road except when the road surface provides insufficient traction.

j) Do not continue to drive an automatic Range Rover if the transmission oil temperature warning light comes on. If this should happen, either position 2 or 1 should be engaged on the main gear selector lever, and if this fails to extinguish the light, low range should be engaged. If the warning light remains on in low range, the vehicle must be stopped and the engine left running with the main selector lever in neutral until the transmission oil cools down and the light is extinguished.

k) Do not allow the engine to idle for long periods with the main gear selector lever in the Park position.

GENERAL ADVICE ON VEHICLE RECOVERY

Should the vehicle become immobile due to loss of traction, the following hints will be of value:–

a) Once the vehicle is stationary, avoid prolonged wheel spin as this will only make matters worse.

b) Try to remove any obstacle i.e. rocks, tree stumps, etc. It will also help to remove any earth or sand that is supporting the weight of the vehicle via the chassis or axles.

c) If the ground is very soft, reduced tyre pressures may help. Remember that this will also reduce ground clearance.

e) Reverse as far as possible and the momentum gained by making a faster second approach may get the vehicle over the obstacle.

f) Brushwood, sacking or any similar material placed in front of the wheels will assist in obtaining traction.

g) If the vehicle has dug itself in, jack it up and build up the ground under the wheels to obtain ground clearance.

These are general guide lines and should help you to make use of the off road capabilities of Land Rovers and Range Rovers. Careful thought and practical experience will usually provide the solution to any problems, but correct driving technique will itself ensure that such instances are kept to a minimum or avoided completely.

USEFUL DATA

	88"	109"	Ninety	One Ten	Range Rover
Approach Angle	46°	49°	47°	50°	45°
Departure Angle	30°	24°	48°	35°	33°
Max. Gradient	45°	45°	45°	45°	45°
Min. Ground Clearance	178mm	209mm	198mm	215mm	190mm
Min. Turning Radius	5.8m	7.15m	5.75m	6.4m	5.65m
Gross Vehicle Weight	2120kg	2710kg 3020kg H.C.P.U.	2400 standard 2550 high load	2950 levelled 3050 standard	2510kg

TOWING CAPACITY

	On Road					Off Road
	88"	109"	Ninety	One Ten	Range Rover	All Models
Unbraked Trailers	500kg	500kg	500kg	500kg	500kg	500kg
Trailers with over-run brakes	2000kg	2000kg	3500kg	3500kg	3500kg	1000kg
4 Wheel trailers with close coupled brakes	4000kg Petrol 3000kg Diesel	4000kg Petrol 3000kg Diesel	4000kg Petrol 3500kg Diesel 4000kg Turbo	4000kg	4000kg	1000kg

LAND ROVER OFFICIAL FACTORY PUBLICATIONS

Land Rover Series 1 Workshop Manual	4291
Land Rover Series 1 1948-53 Parts Catalogue	4051
Land Rover Series 1 1954-58 Parts Catalogue	4107
Land Rover Series 1 Instruction Manual	4277
Land Rover Series 1 & II Diesel Instruction Manual	4343
Land Rover Series II & IIA Workshop Manual	AKM8159
Land Rover Series II & Early IIA Bonneted Control Parts Catalogue	605957
Land Rover Series IIA Bonneted Control Parts Catalogue	RTC9840CC
Land Rover Series IIA, III & 109 V8 Optional Equipment Parts Catalogue	RTC9842CE
Land Rover Series IIA/IIB Instruction Manual	LSM64 IM
Land Rover Series III Workshop Manual	AKM3648
Land Rover Series III Workshop Manual V8 Supplement (edn. 2)	AKM8022
Land Rover Series III 88, 109 & 109 V8 Parts Catalogue	RTC9841CE
Land Rover Series III Owners' Manual 1971-81	607324B
Land Rover Series III Owners' Manual 1981-85	AKM8155
Land Rover 90/110 & Defender Workshop Manual 1983-92	SLR621ENWM
Land Rover Defender Workshop Manual 1993-95	LDAWMEN93
(Covering petrol 2.25, 2.5, 3.5 V8 & diesel 2.25, 2.5, 2.5 Turbo, 200 Tdi)	
Land Rover Defender 300 Tdi Workshop Manual 1996-98	LRL 0097 ENG
Land Rover Defender Td5 Workshop Manual & Supplements 1999-2005 on	LRL 0410BB
Land Rover Defender Electrical Manual Td5 99-05 on & 300Tdi 02-05 on	LRD5EHBB
Contains YVB 101670, VDL 100170, LRL 0452 ENG & LRL 0389 ENG	
Land Rover 110 Parts Catalogue 1983-86	RTC9863CE
Land Rover Defender Parts Catalogue 1987-2001 on	STC9021CC
Land Rover 90 • 110 Owners' Handbook 1983-1990	LSM0054
Land Rover 90 • 110 • 130 Owners' Handbook 1991-Feb. 1994	LHAHBEN93
Land Rover 90 • 110 • 130 Owners' Handbook March 1994-1998	LRL0087ENG/2
Discovery Workshop Manual 1990-94 (petrol 3.5, 3.9, Mpi & diesel 200 Tdi)	SJR900ENWM
Discovery Workshop Manual 1995-98 (petrol 2.0 Mpi, 3.9, 4.0 V8 & diesel 300 Tdi)	LRL0079BB
Discovery Series II Workshop Manual 1999-02 (petrol 4.0 V8 & diesel Td5)	VDR 100090
Discovery Parts Catalogue 1989-98 (2.0 Mpi, 3.5, 3.9 V8 & 200 Tdi & 300 Tdi)	RTC9947CF
Discovery Owners' Handbook 1990-1991 (petrol 3.5 & diesel 200 Tdi)	SJR820ENHB90
Freelander Workshop Manual 1998-2000 (petrol 1.8 and diesel 2.0)	LRL0144

Land Rover Military (Lightweight) Series III Parts Catalogue
Land Rover Military (Lightweight) Series III User Manual   608180
Land Rover 101 1 Tonne Forward Control Workshop Manual   RTC9120
Land Rover 101 1 Tonne Forward Control Parts Catalogue   608294B
Land Rover 101 1 Tonne Forward Control User Manual   608239

Range Rover Workshop Manual 1970-85 (petrol 3.5)   AKM3630
Range Rover Workshop Manual 1986-89   SRR660ENWM &
    (petrol 3.5 & diesel 2.4 Turbo VM & 2.5 Turbo VM)   LSM180WS4 Ed 2
Range Rover Workshop Manual 1990-94
    (petrol 3.9, 4.2 & diesel 2.5 Turbo VM, 200 Tdi)   LHAWMENA02
Range Rover Workshop Manual 1995-01 (petrol 4.0, 4.6 & BMW 2.5 diesel) VDR 100370
Range Rover Parts Catalogue 1970-85 (petrol 3.5)   RTC9846CH
Range Rover Parts Catalogue 1986-91
    (petrol 3.5, 3.9 & diesel 2.4 Turbo VM & 2.5 Turbo VM)   RTC9908CB
Range Rover Parts Catalogue 1992-94 MY & 95 MY Classic
    (petrol 3.9, 4.2 & diesel 2.5 Turbo VM, 200 Tdi & 300 Tdi) RTC9961CB
Range Rover Owners' Handbook 1970-80 (petrol 3.5)   606917
Range Rover Owners' Handbook 1981-82 (petrol 3.5)   AKM 8139
Range Rover Owners' Handbook 1983-85 (petrol 3.5)   LSM 0001HB
Range Rover Owners' Handbook 1986-87 (petrol 3.5 & diesel 2.4 Turbo VM) LSM 129HB
Range Rover Owners' Handbook 1988-89 (petrol 3.5 & diesel 2.4 Turbo VM) SRR600ENHB

Engine Overhaul Manuals for Land Rover & Range Rover
300 Tdi Engine, R380 Manual Gearbox & LT230T Transfer Gearbox Overhaul Manuals LRL 003, 070 & 081
Petrol Engine V8 3.5, 3.9, 4.0, 4.2 & 4.6 Overhaul Manuals   LRL 004 & 164

Land Rover/Range Rover Driving Techniques   LR 369
Working in the Wild - Manual for Africa   SMR 684MI
Winching in Safety   SMR 699MI

Owners' Workhop Manuals
Land Rover 2 / 2A / 3 1959-1983 Owners' Workshop Manual
Land Rover 90, 110 & Defender 1983-1995 Owners' Workshop Manual

From Land Rover specialists or, in case of difficulty, direct from the distributors:
Brooklands Books Ltd., PO Box 146, Cobham, Surrey, KT11 1LG, England.
Telephone: 01932 865051 Fax: 01932 868803
e-mail sales@brooklands-books.com www.brooklands-books.com
Brooklands Books Australia, 3/37-39 Green Street, Banksmeadow, NSW 2019, Australia
Phone: 2 9695 7055 Fax: 2 9695 7355
Car Tech, 39966 Grand Avenue, North Branch, MN 55056, USA
Telephone: 800 551 4754 & 651 277 1200 Fax: 651 277 1203

Printed and distributed by
Brooklands Books Ltd., P.O. Box 146, Cobham, Surrey KT11 1LG, England
Phone: 01932 865051 Fax: 01932 868803
E-mail: sales@brooklands-books.com   www.brooklands-books.com

ISBN 1 85520 2867   Part No. LR 369   200/06Z6   Ref: B-LRDTHH
Printed in China